The Essential JIM BRICKMAN

Arranged by Dan Coates

Volume 2: Songs

Contents

DAN COATES® is a registered trademark of Alfred Publishing Co., Inc.

© MMVII by Alfred Publishing Co., Inc.

All rights reserved. Printed in USA.

ISBN-10: 0-7390-4848-1
ISBN-13: 978-0-7390-4848-1

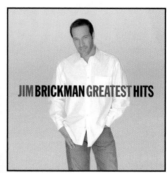

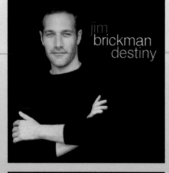

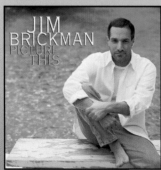

BY HEART

Written by Jim Brickman and Hollye Leven
Arranged by Dan Coates

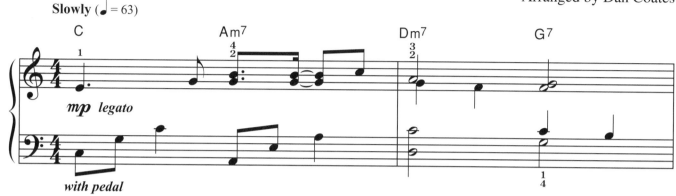

1. Hold me close,___ ba - by,___ please.
2. When you go,___ I'll stop___ the___ clock.

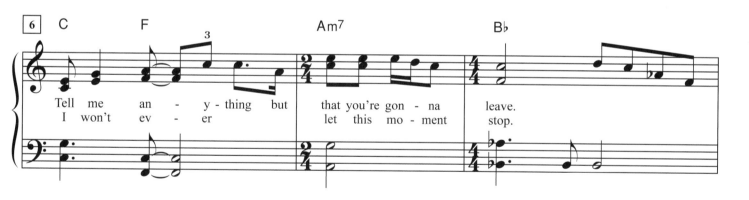

Tell me an - y - thing but that you're gon - na leave.
I won't ev - er let this mo - ment stop.

As I kiss___ this fal - len tear,___ I pro - mise you I will be___
Time is steal - in' you from me,___ but it can nev - er take this mem - o -

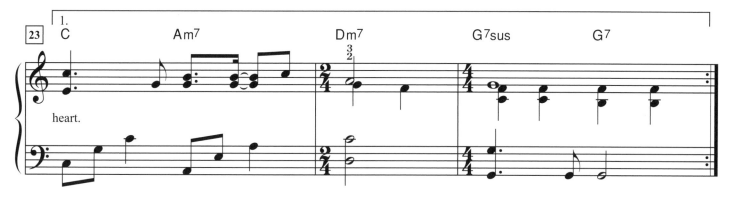

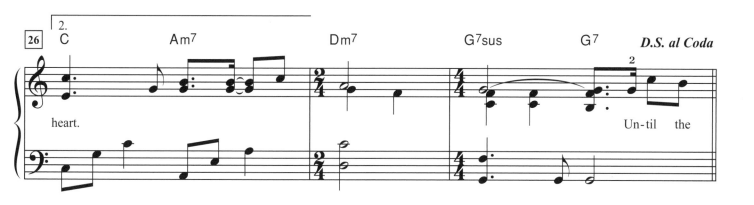

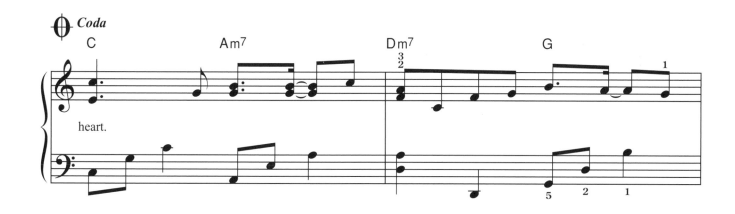

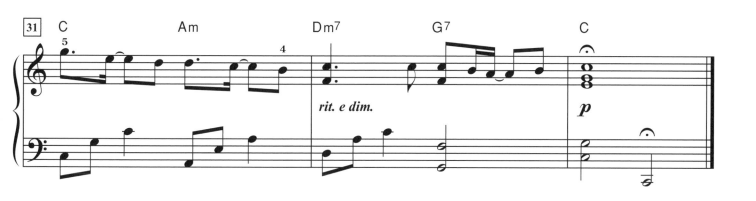

AFTER ALL THESE YEARS

Words and Music by David Grow
Arranged by Dan Coates

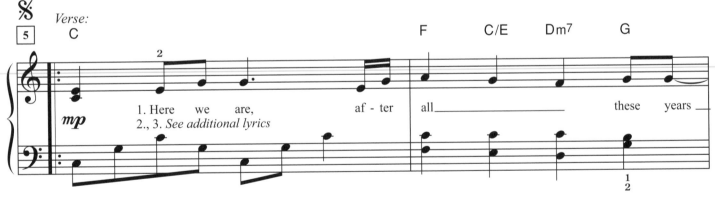

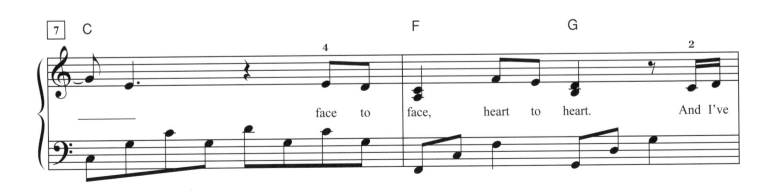

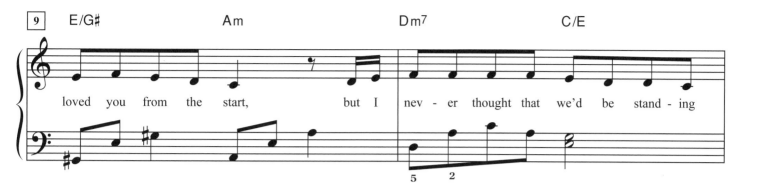

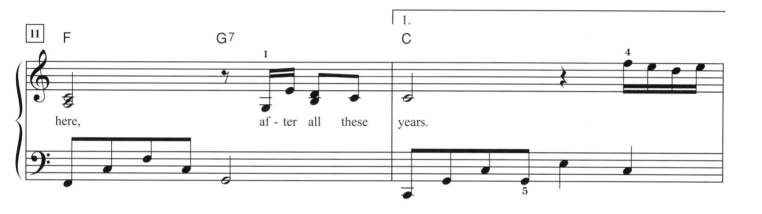

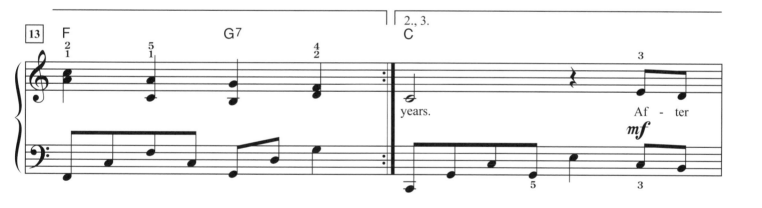

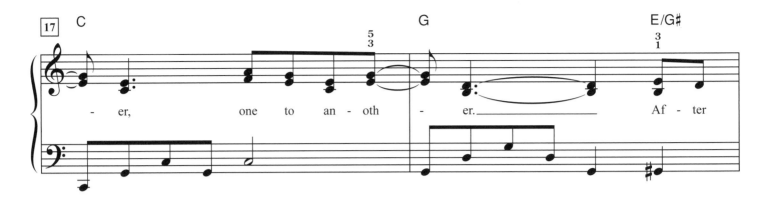

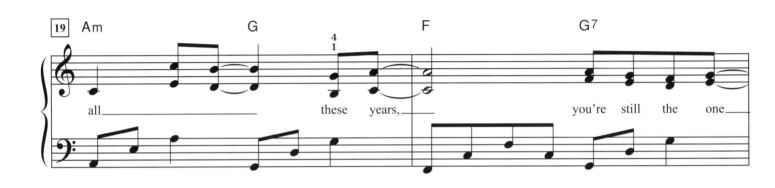

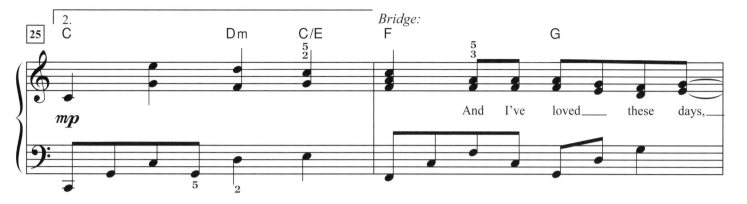

And I've loved____ these days,____

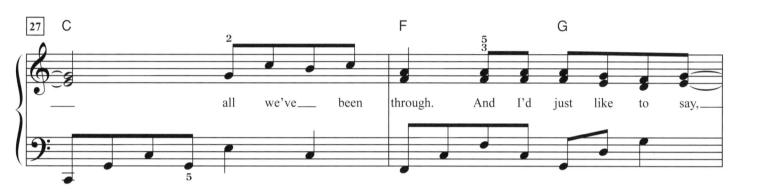

____ all we've____ been through. And I'd just like to say,____

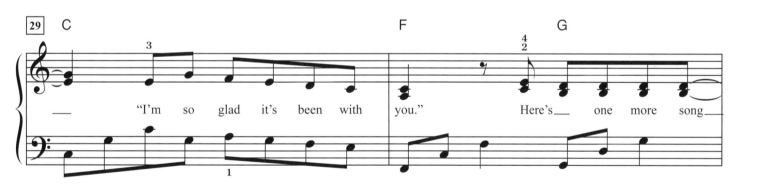

____ "I'm so glad it's been with you." Here's____ one more song____

____ from the heart____ for the laugh-ter and____ the tears,____

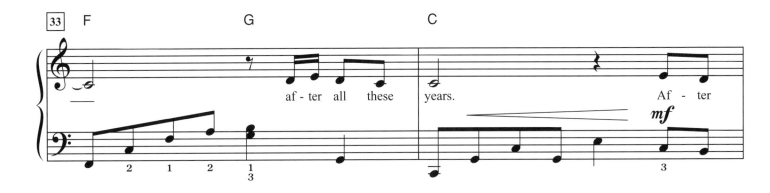

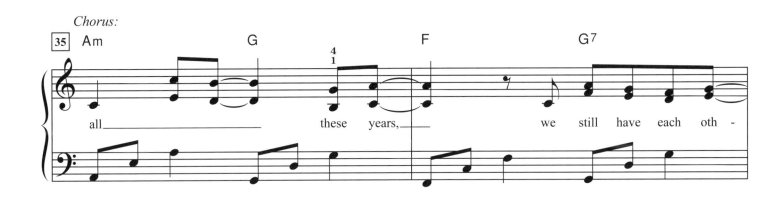

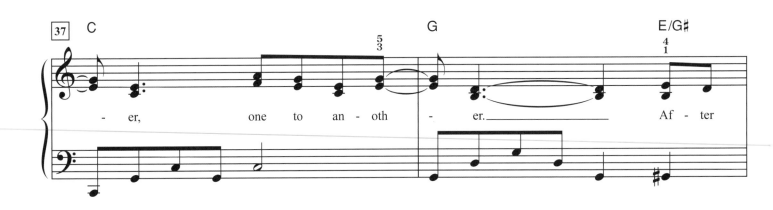

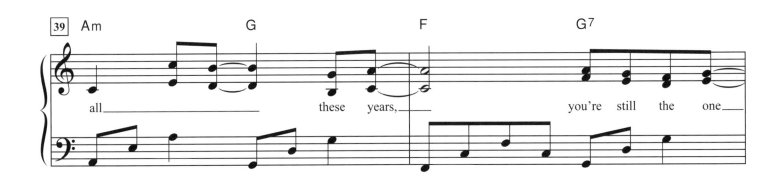

Verse 2:
Here we are,
With another song to sing.
All these days passed us by
As we watched our childhood fly.
And I'm still the one
To share your hopes and fears,
After all these years.
(To Chorus:)

Verse 3:
Here we are,
With another bridge to cross,
Face to face, heart to heart.
And I've loved you from the start,
But I never thought that
We'd be standing here,
After all these years.
(To Chorus:)

BEAUTIFUL (AS YOU)

Words and Music by Jim Brickman,
Jack Kugell and Jamie Jones
Arranged by Dan Coates

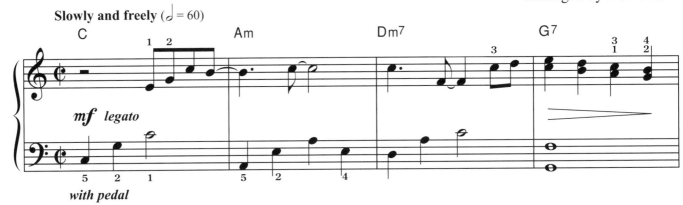

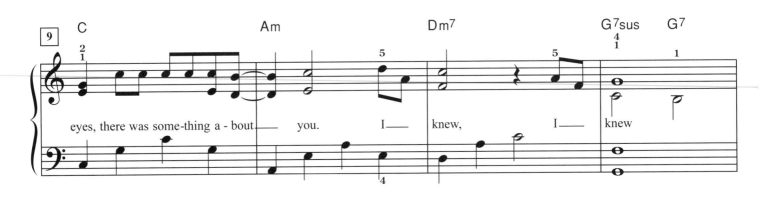

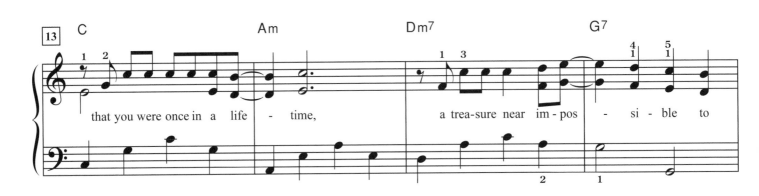

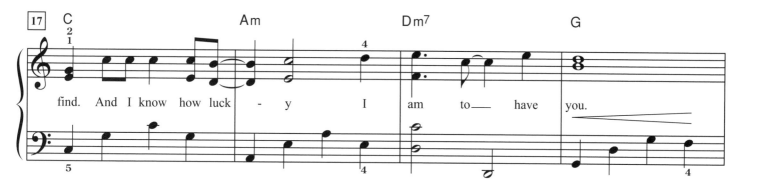

Chorus:

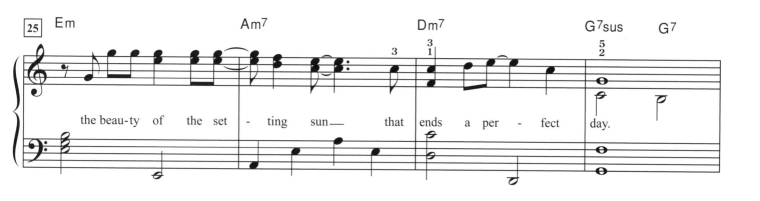

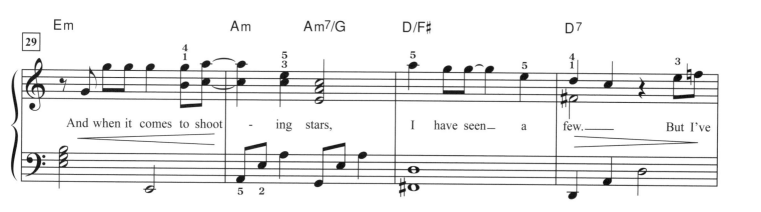

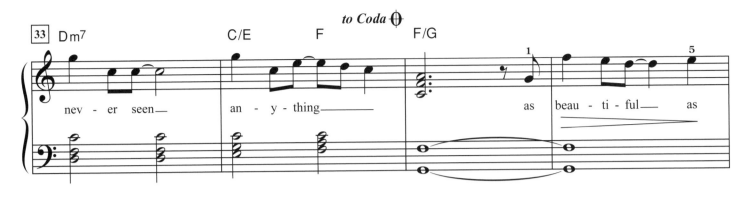

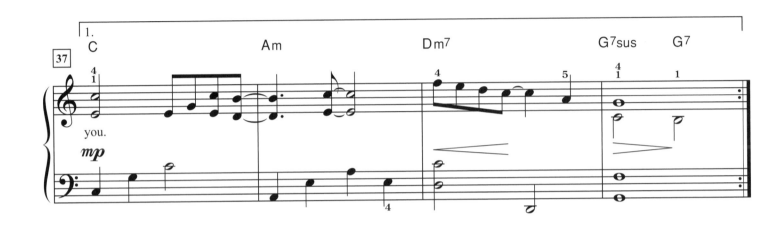

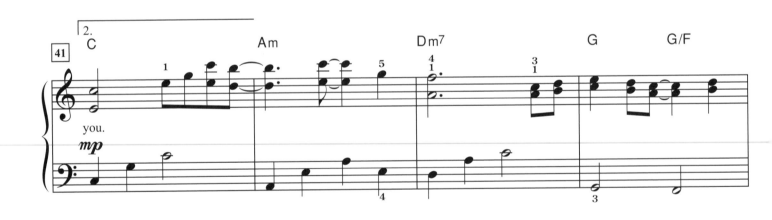

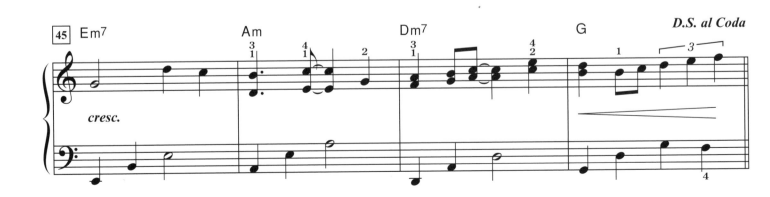

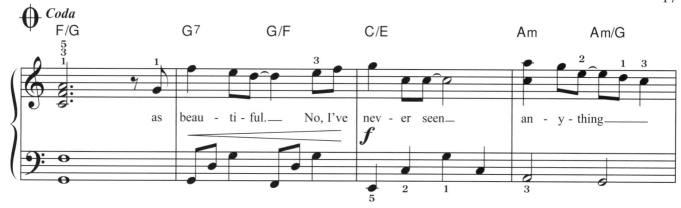

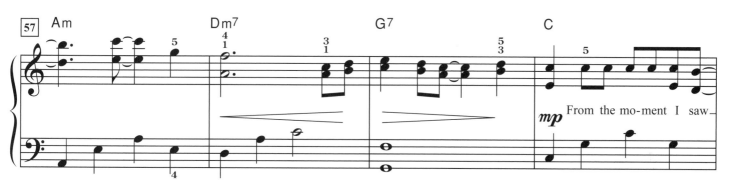

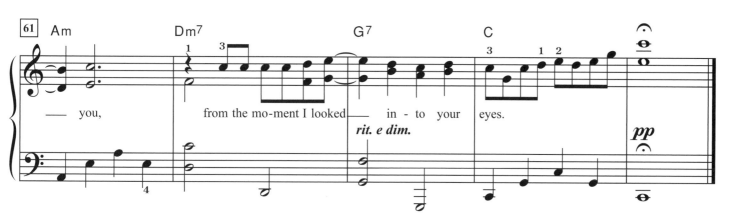

Verse 2:
Holding you in my arms,
No one else has fit so perfectly.
I could dance forever with you, with you.
And at the stroke of midnight,
Please forgive me if I can't let go,
'Cause I never dreamed I'd find
A Cinderella of my own.
(To Chorus:)

DESTINY

Words and Music by Jim Brickman,
Sean Hosen, and Dane Deviller
Arranged by Dan Coates

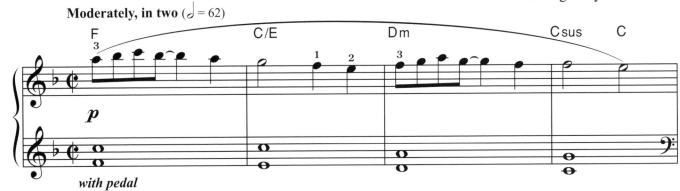

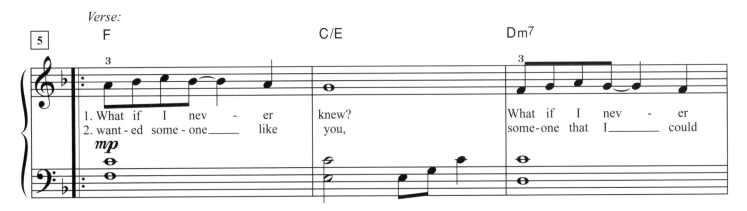

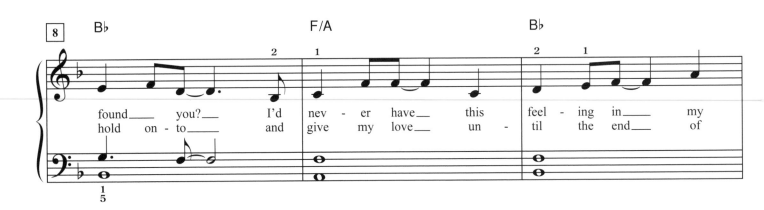

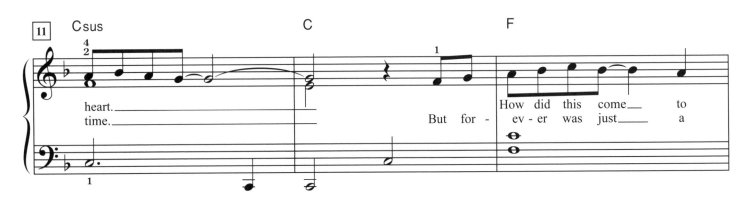

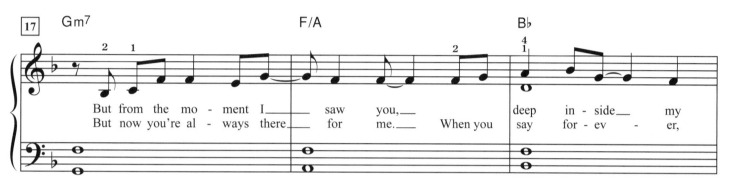

Chorus:

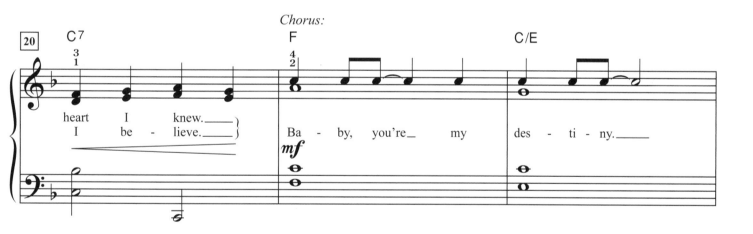

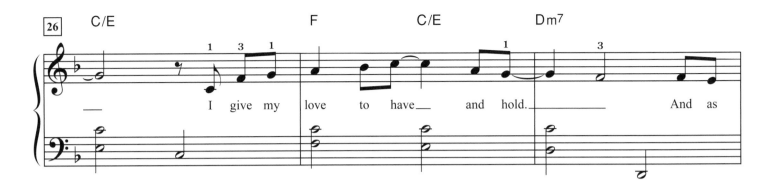

I give my love to have__ and hold.__ And as

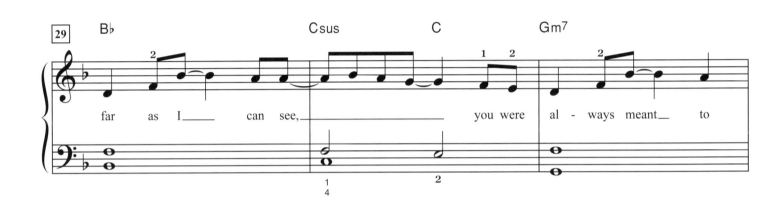

far as I____ can see,_____ you were al - ways meant__ to

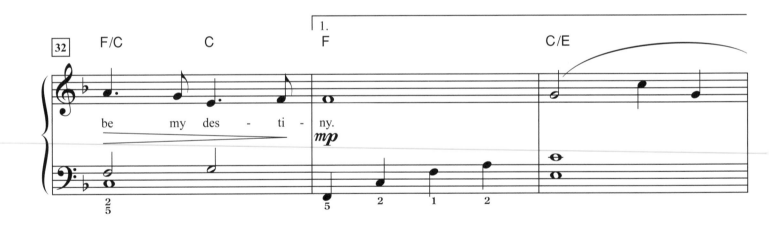

be my des - ti - ny. *mp*

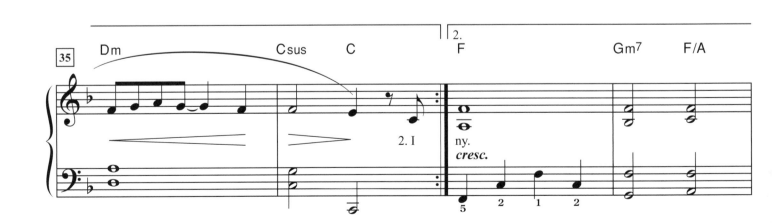

2. I ny. *cresc.*

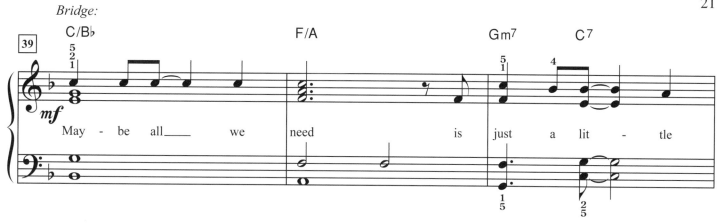

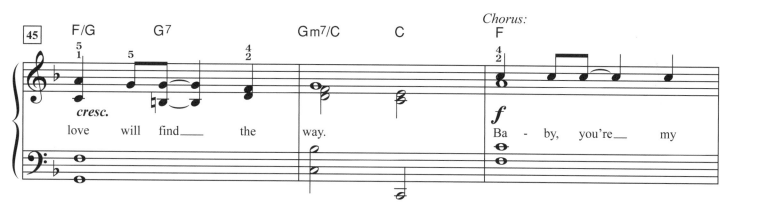

THE GIFT

Words and Music by
Jim Brickman and Tom Douglas
Arranged by Dan Coates

24

I'M AMAZED

Words and Music by
David Grow and Victoria Shaw
Arranged by Dan Coates

THE LOVE I FOUND IN YOU

Words and Music by
Jim Brickman, Tom Douglas,
Brad Warren and Brett Warren
Arranged by Dan Coates

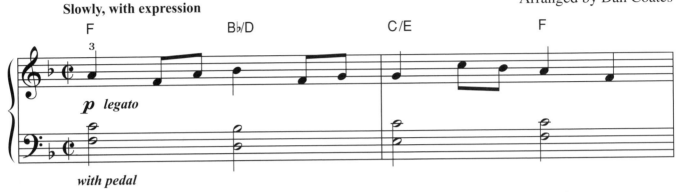

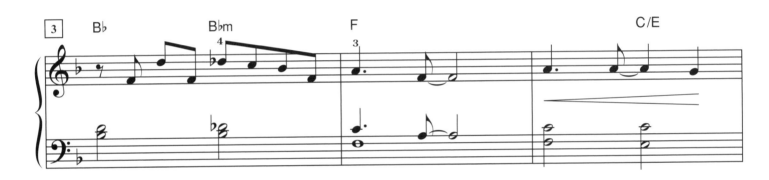

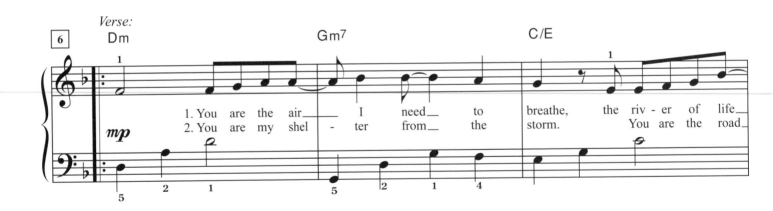

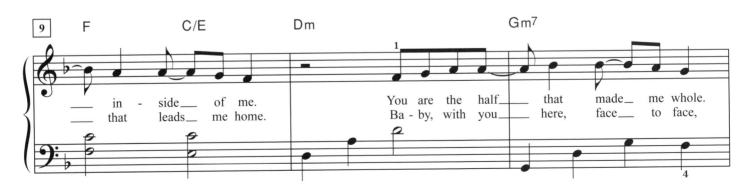

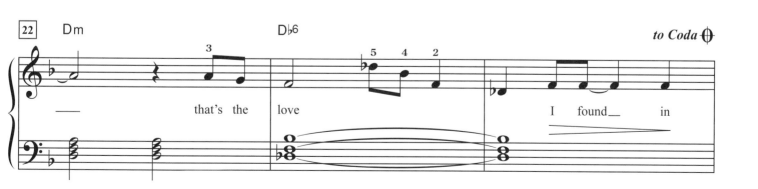

32

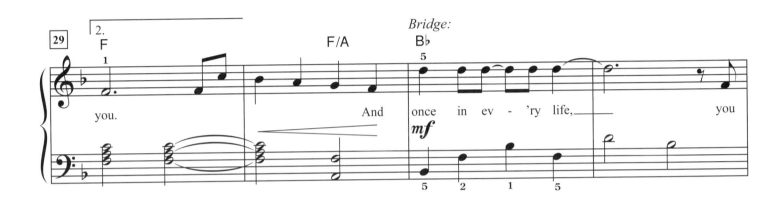

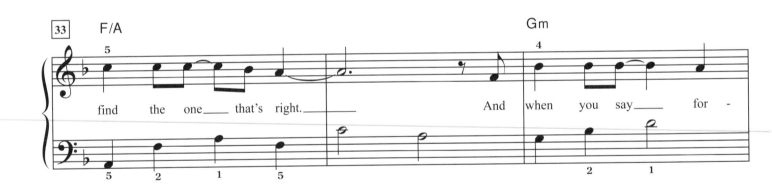

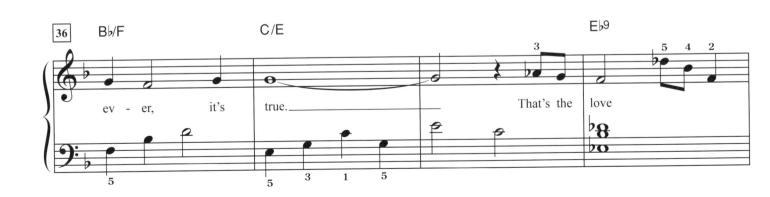

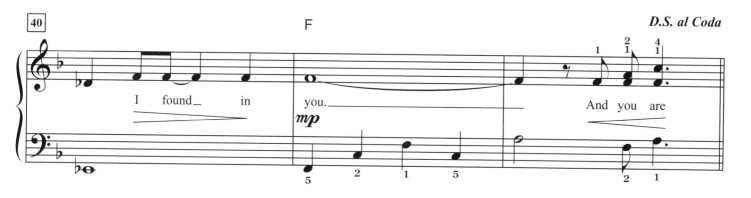

D.S. al Coda

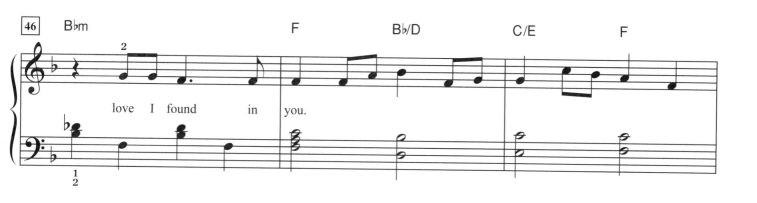

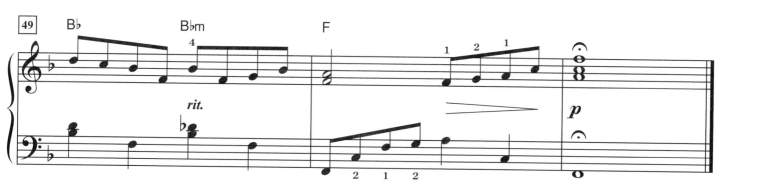

LOVE OF MY LIFE

Words and Music by
Jim Brickman and Tom Douglas
Arranged by Dan Coates

35

36

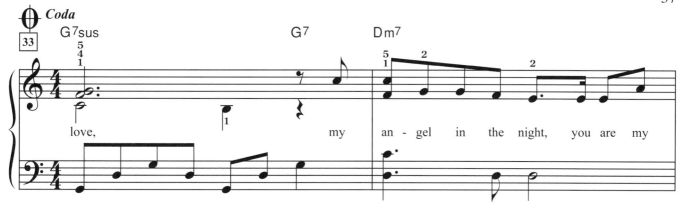

love, my an-gel in the night, you are my

love, the love of my life.

Verse 2:
Now, here you are,
With midnight closing in.
You take my hand as our shadows dance,
With moonlight on your skin.
I look in your eyes.
I'm lost inside your kiss.
I think if I'd never met you
About all the things I'd missed.
Sometimes it's so hard to believe
When a love can be so strong,
And faith gave me the strength
And kept me holding on.
(To Chorus:)

MY ANGEL

Words and Music by
Jim Brickman and Tom Douglas
Arranged by Dan Coates

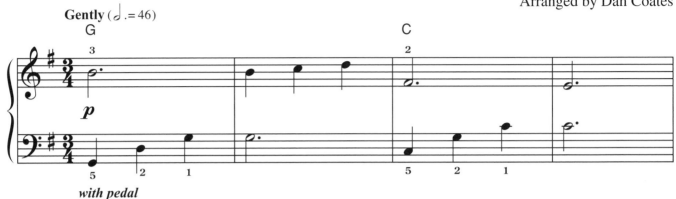

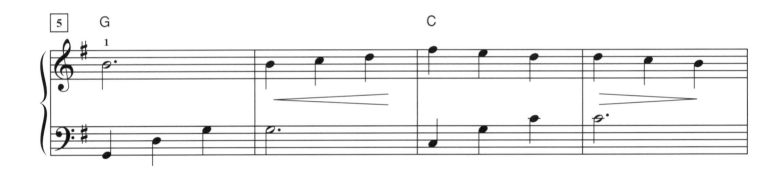

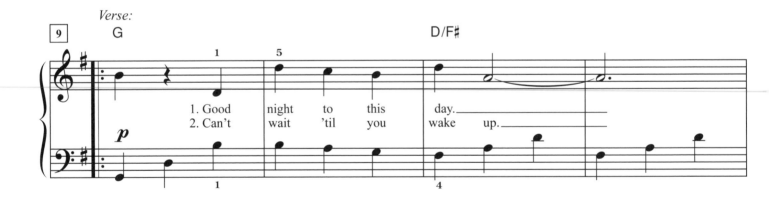

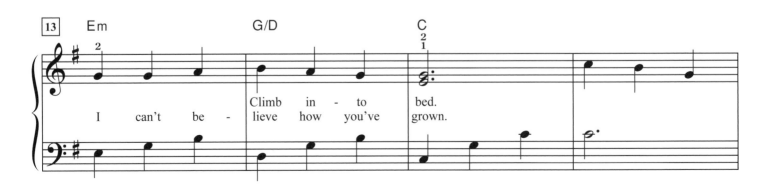

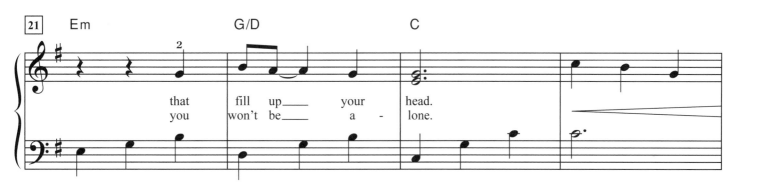

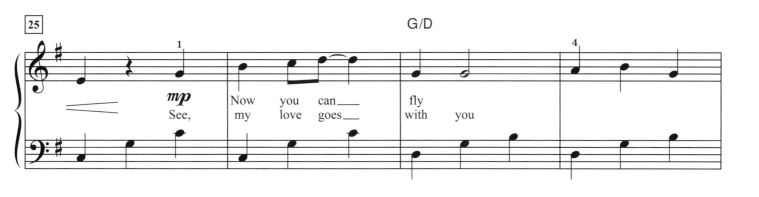

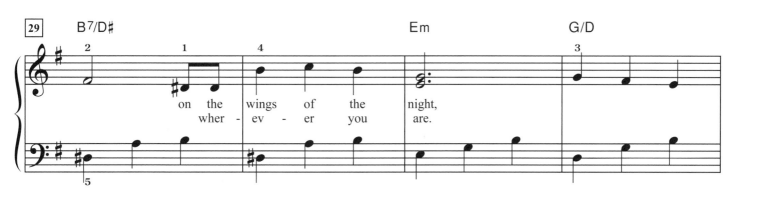

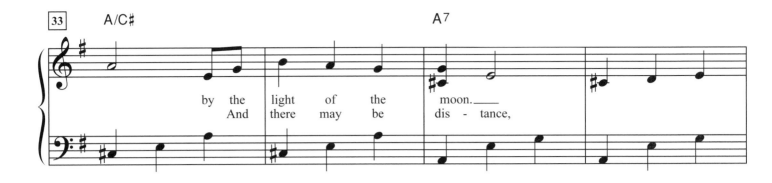

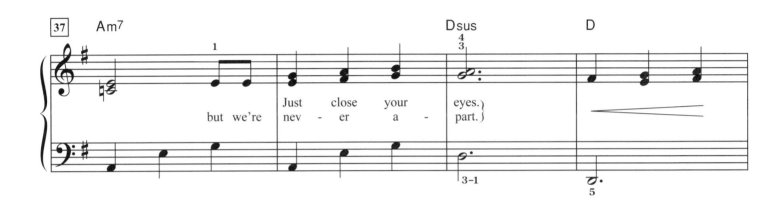

Chorus:

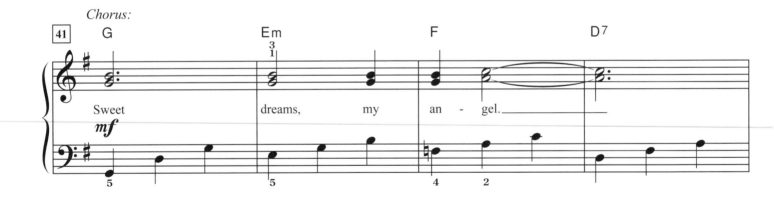

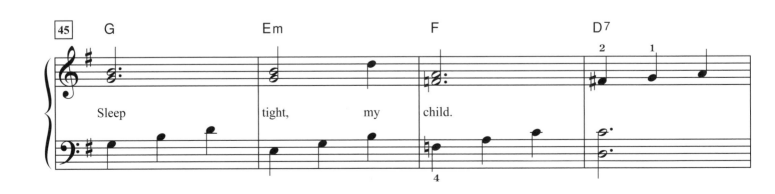

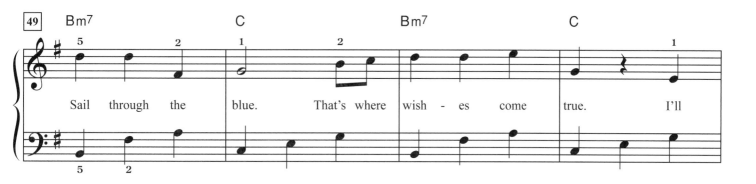

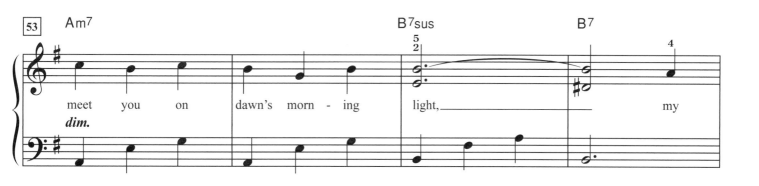

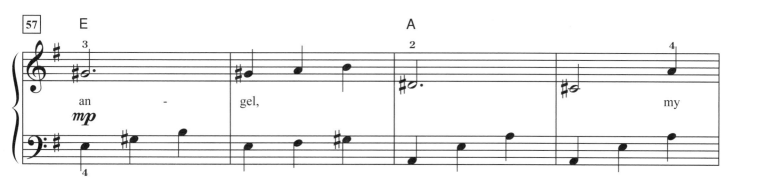

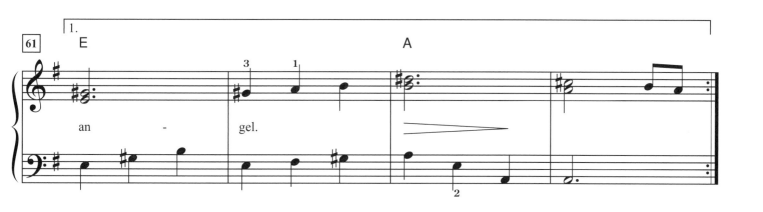

42

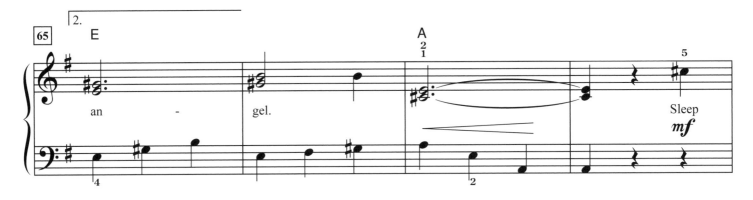

an - gel.
Sleep
mf

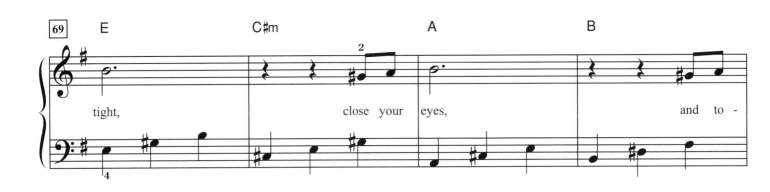

tight,
close your eyes,
and to-

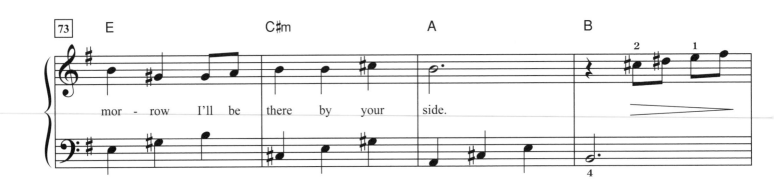

mor - row I'll be there by your side.

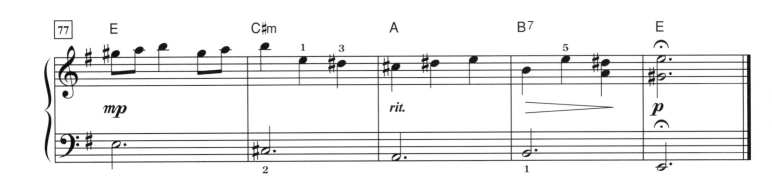

mp
rit.
p

WHEN IT SNOWS

Words and Music by
Jim Brickman and Darrell Brown
Arranged by Dan Coates

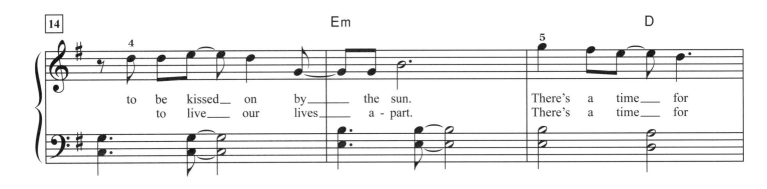

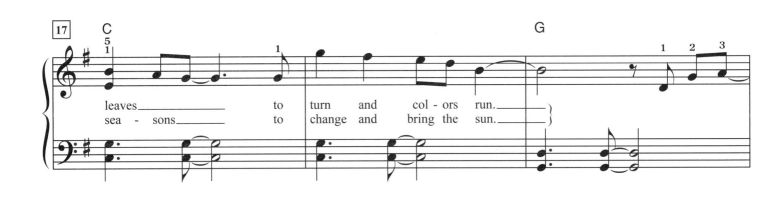

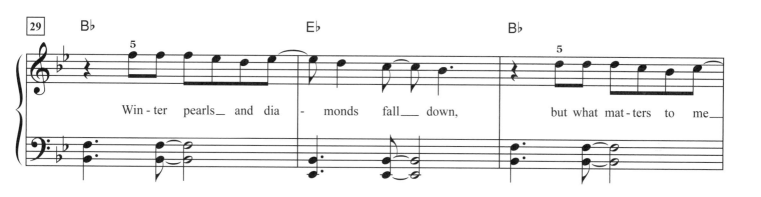

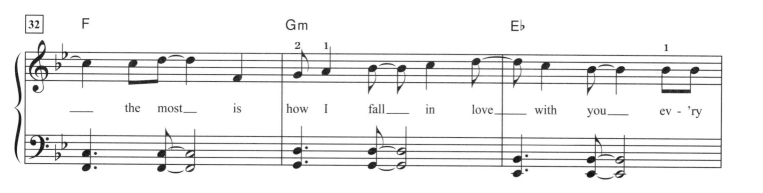

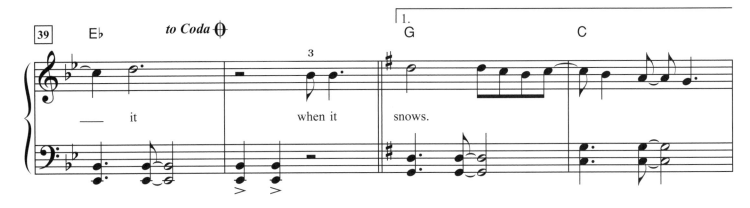

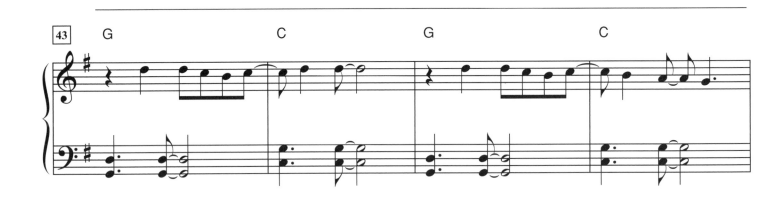

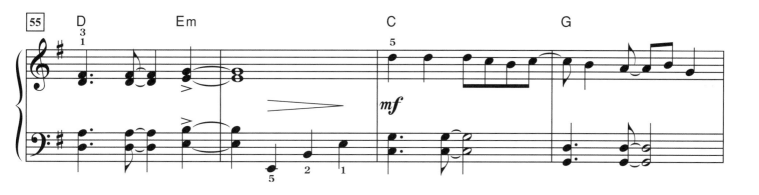

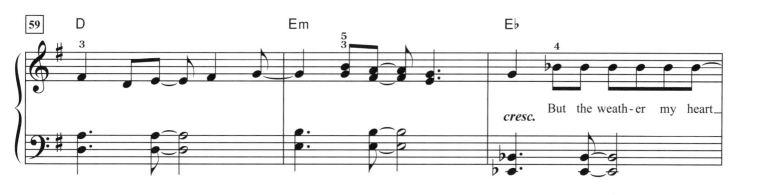

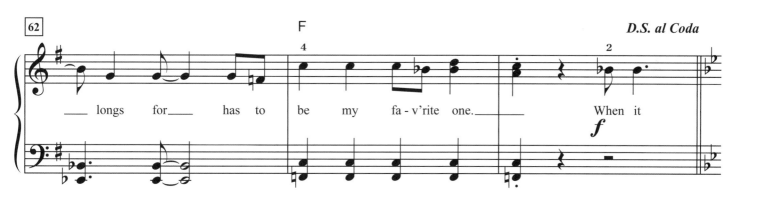

SIMPLE THINGS

Words and Music by
Jim Brickman, Darrell Brown
and Beth Nielsen Chapman
Arranged by Dan Coates

Moderately, with a steady beat ($\bullet$ = 92)

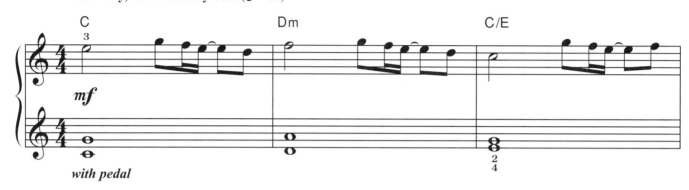

50

I love the way— the sim-ple things, the sim-ple things just are.

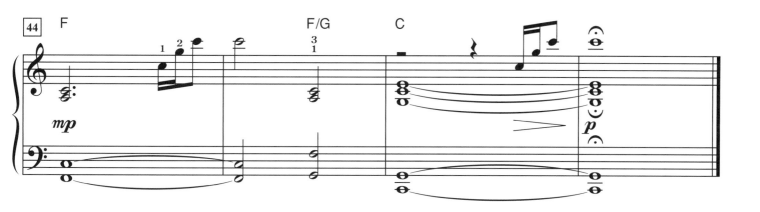

Verse 2:
So, here we go.
Let's just dance;
Teach my soul to take this chance.
Put my heart
In your hands.
Out of all the moments that we leave behind,
Turn around and tell me, baby, we'll remember:

Chorus 2:
The thunder and the rain;
The way you say my name.
After all the clouds go by,
The simple things remain.
The sun, the moon, the stars;
The beating of two hearts.
How I love the simple things,
The simple things just are.

Chorus 3:
The ocean and the sky;
The way we feel tonight.
I know that it's the love
That brings the simple things to light.
The sun, the moon, the stars;
The beating of two hearts.
I love the way the simple things,
The simple things just are.

TO HEAR YOU SAY YOU LOVE ME

Words and Music by
Jim Brickman and Victoria Shaw
Arranged by Dan Coates

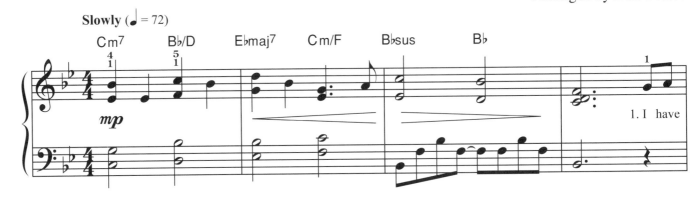

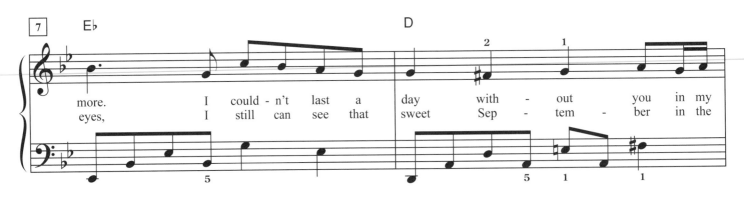

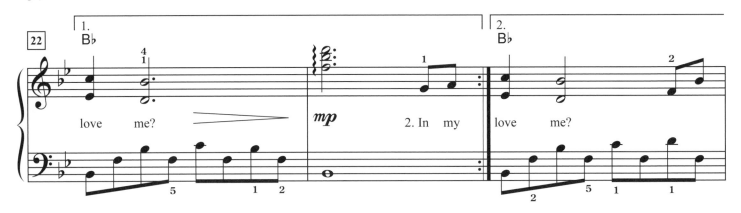

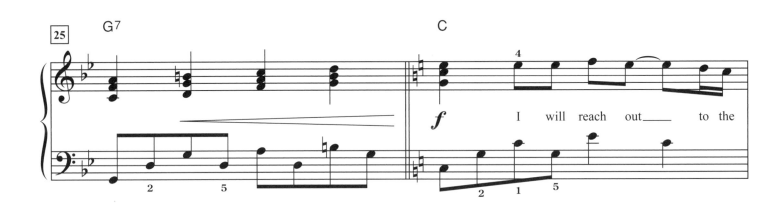

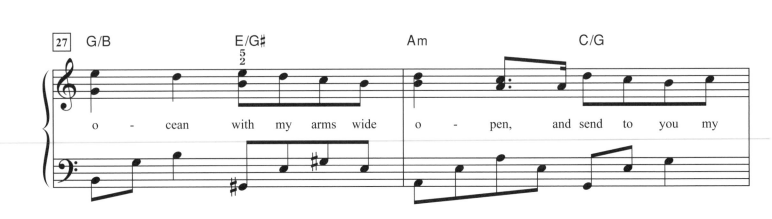

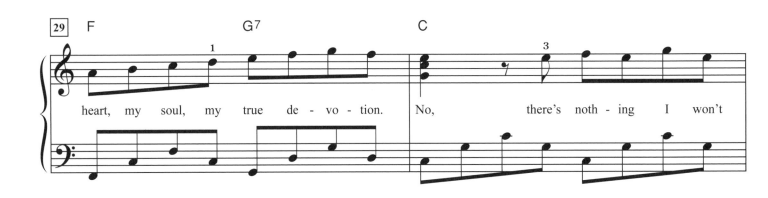

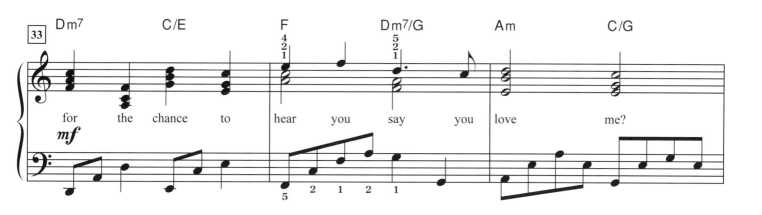

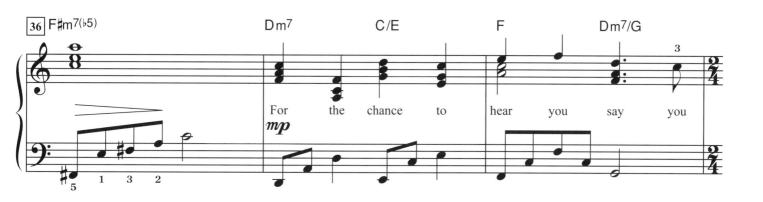

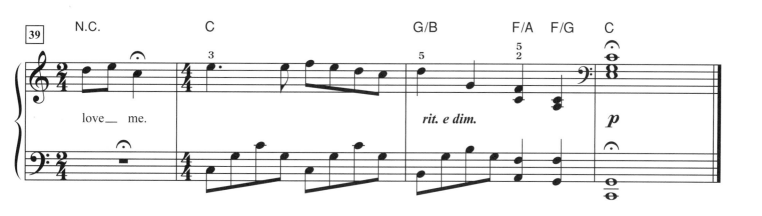

VALENTINE

Words and Music by
Jim Brickman and Jack Kugell
Arranged by Dan Coates

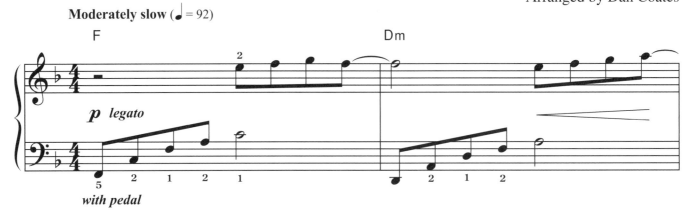

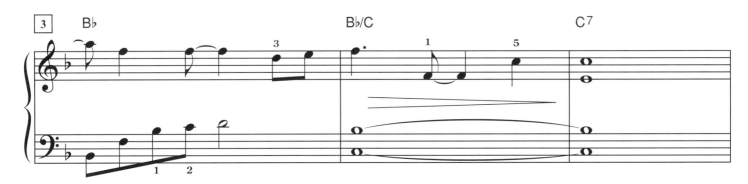

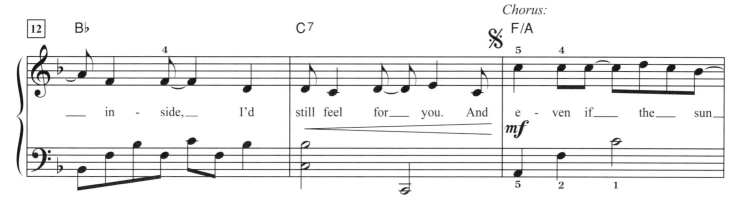

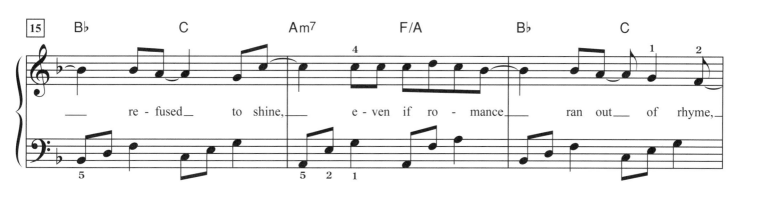

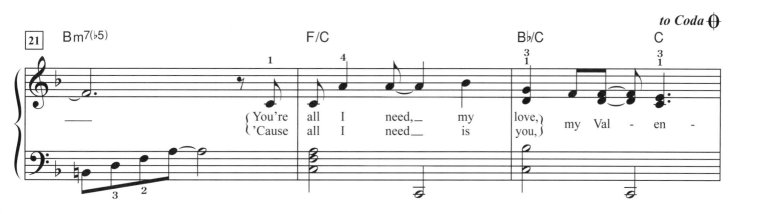

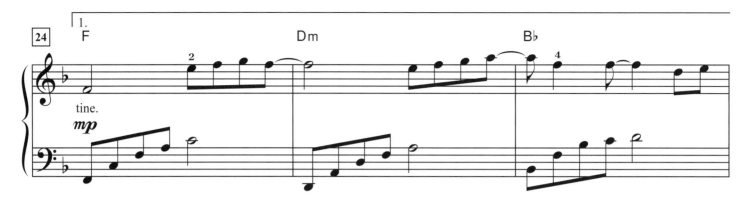

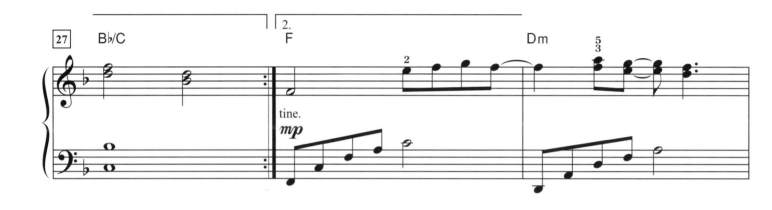

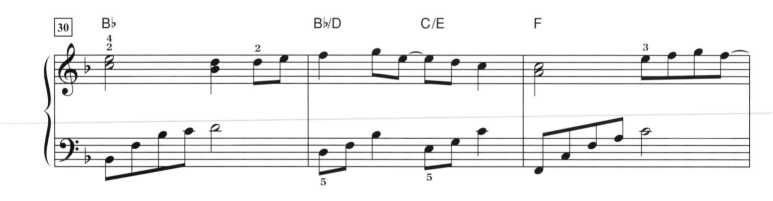

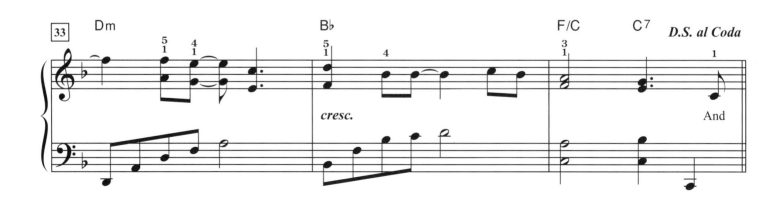

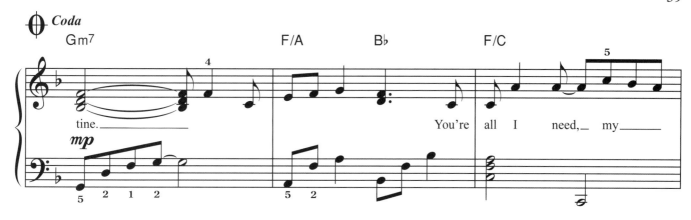

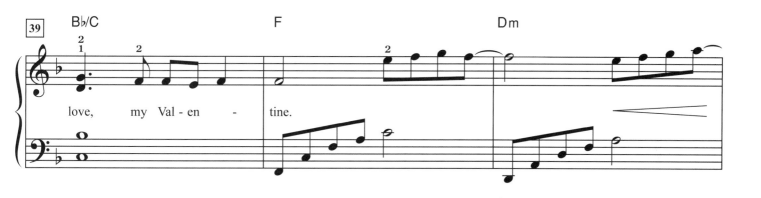

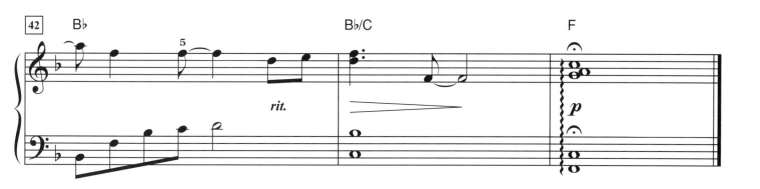

Verse 2:
All of my life,
I have been waiting for all you give to me.
You've opened my eyes
And shown me how to love unselfishly.
I've dreamed of this a thousand times before,
But in my dreams I couldn't love you more.
I will give you my heart until the end of time.
You're all I need, my love,
My Valentine.

YOUR LOVE

Words and Music by Jim Brickman,
Sean Hosein and Dane Deviller
Arranged by Dan Coates

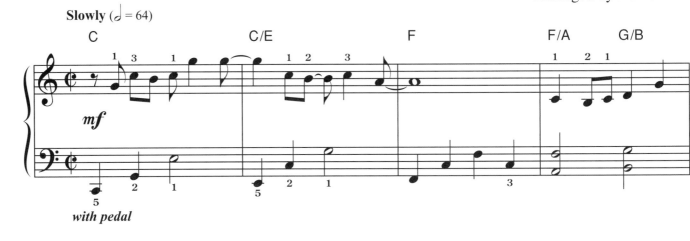

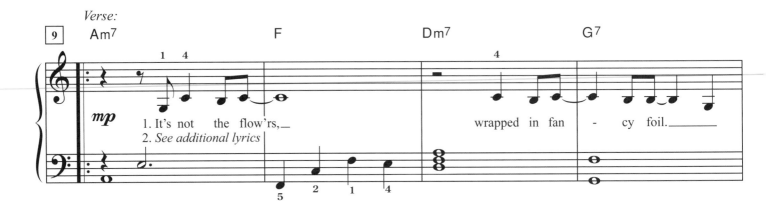

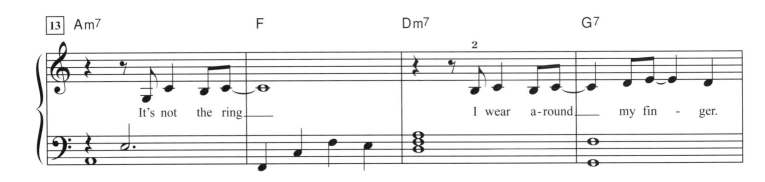

Verse 2:
In your arms,
I found a strength inside me.
And in your eyes,
There's a light to guide me.
I would be lost without you.
And all that my heart could ever want
Has come true.
(To Chorus:)